DYS

My journey of

Firdos Tarannum

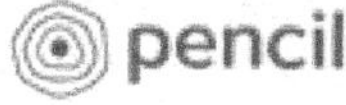
pencil

ISBN 978-93-5610-901-8
© Firdos Tarannum 2022
Published in India 2022 by Pencil

A brand of
One Point Six Technologies Pvt. Ltd.
123, Building J2, Shram Seva Premises,
Wadala Truck Terminal, Wadala (E)
Mumbai 400037, Maharashtra, INDIA
E connect@thepencilapp.com
W www.thepencilapp.com

DISCLAIMER: *The opinions expressed in this book are those of the authors and do not purport to reflect the views of the Publisher.*

Author biography

Firdos Tarannum is a teacher , with a degree in bachelor of science.She completed her school education in holy family school of Sindhanur, and completed her science field education in a renowned college called smj pu college, sindhanur.

Firdos Tarannum always admired of educating herself and others around her , she lived her life to the fullest before marriage and Alhamdulillah her every dream of educating the children completed.She taught some religious topics to the students of an islamic school where her parents studied which was a stepping stone of her teaching field, she completed the degree and started teaching in the same year immersing herself into two different roles everyday.She also gave tuition classes for the kids and also actively participated in courses of Islamic organisation held every week and ten days in summer months She also served as a science teacher in her own learned school for a year , which was a proud moment for her teacher seeing their student sitting with them on the same post at such an early stage.Lockdown throughout the world stopped the teaching of many teachers and one among them was firdos too.She completed her degree on the other hand successfully just before lockdown.During the times of lockdown she used them in a good way by handling around motivational or councilling sessions as her second dream is to help people with her words which have an immense effect on one's mind as people are often get themselves in depression and stress. She got married and gave birth to a wonderful son in a year of marriage itself Alhamdulillah. But this didn't stop her from completing her dreams. Tarannum is a housewife and a mother, who recently inspired herself to write the books after finding her love towards studies, she loved reading and was always appreciated for her work either for her teaching of 3 years or a councilling sessions.With her support of her spouse she now balances her work,child and book Her only dream is to, then to try have a weekend class for neighborhood children and often conduct workshop for dealing with mental health. At the same time , keeping herself educated and learn something everyday and teach something often so that this journey of her is continued by her children in sha Allah.If one loves something truly then it is the sole responsibility of oneself to take care of surroundings and their talent as well while fulfilling all their responsibilities

CONTENTS

MY FEELINGS

When i attended the workshop, i made some good friends but never thought, i would make friends who are very elder to me. When i registered for 10 days workshop, i searched about the resort, and did packing accordingly. All i planned was to make good friends. Then, when I reached there on the first day, i realised, I was the youngest among all, just like a fresher, but this didn't stopped me from interacting with them.

I first met the coach, greeted him and then met two ladies, where I introduced myself and then there, i saw a woman walking in a hurried manner like she was late, a scarf on, a hijab, Specks and her long running legs she was a Lawyer, was half of her age and height as well. she introduced herself and said "Am a lawyer. since, 20 years hearing this my eyes widened and my mind started to calculate her age. looking at her deeply thinking, is she married! who came with her? etc. but all the questions stopped popping as our conversation increased she was in the same block as me, we prayed, laughed, ate and lived together she still thinks me as her daughter

On the first day, there were a lot of people, i met with interesting backgrounds & professions like teacher housewife reporters, lecturers, job holders, Lawyer, doctor, physiotherapist, Social worker-etc

I stayed in a room with two beautiful women One was a maintainer of health & she was quite strict and this made most of us wake up early for walk and exercise.

I had an activity to share with a woman who was a grandmother, i couldn't believe, that people at this age attended to change themselves for good. Sadly, we notice most old people being Stubborn, not changing anything within and around them but, this was not the case, every participant had a rough and hard experience of life and i thanked Allah that i met people like them.many of the participants were regular attenders of the workshop and thus bonding between them was easily noticeable . There were two families with kids who were in resort with us, and those kids and their laughter made the atmosphere, a lot more positive.

There were several groups during tea breaks & lunch sessions, one was the coach & one participant, the other group was random one with random talks. one was a group of seriousness, discussing all the topics they learned in the session .one group was overly excited for getting phone during break one group was with the family checking & serving them. on the other it was me, shifting constantly my groups fo interact with others ,As I promised myself that this time would be break from everything.

A wonderful sight to look after was sitting Near a pool of Fishes, spending at least a few minutes just watching them with recitation of the Quran. That time spent everyday with nature was helping me to discover myself. The silence was asking me, "what next thing do i want to do in life now? what exciting turn will my life take from here?"

on the last day, every participant was getting certified & when my dad's name was announced , i opened my camera for a video. when my dad held his mike and said that it was a little difficult for him to understand english, yet he managed to learn and make some new friends. he became a little emotional while Saying So, i stopped my camera because I wanted to witness this moment that the man who is pillar of my life was crying and this workshop taught me the biggest lesson that A FATHER IS ALSO A HUMAN WITH EMOTIONS

I always lived with a perspective in my mind, that i should respect and serve him, but, his day broke every boundary and i realised that he is the man with whom I should share my decisions, opinions and my feelings too. Till today i love my father, I miss him everyday after getting married, .

Till today, i call him and talk to him and let him have an update.

I am thankful for this workshop and for that moment that made me realise that he is just having a role to accept and fulfill his responsibility.

other than that, he is just a man, a human with feelings and emotions to express.

The workshop took a deep turn when every participant started to open their old pages of hurtful & guilt memories of life. I was so shocked to see that everyone had Some major issues to deal with like a mother feared about raising their kids without a father, a wife upset with her husband, young adults forcing themselves to live without enjoying, father sacrificing their desires for children, brother & his disputes with family etc.

I looked upon my life and thanked Allah that my problems were not even a cent percent major, i came here to enjoy but what a turn my life took and it made me learn & be thankful.Nobody believed that i was a teacher with two years of experience, everybody thought i got more of achievements at such a young age. I had no more goals to achieve after this workshop, because i was living my life to the fullest by studying and teaching, all my dream was to teach & i was doing it. In a month, my studies were about to end & job too because i wanted the job for a year.

The workshop provided me with a new goal. whatever i learnt i must share it with others. My dream goal is to help others with their mental health problems because every smile is important.

HOW IT STARTED

How it started-

A session for NLP (Neuro linguistic programming) was carried out in our town to introduce it among people. The coach gave the audience an activity and asked about the lessons we learnt through it, i was the last among all to share my opinion. Almost everyone gave the same opinion and my mind thought to give the same response as them but at last i gave my h honest answer which i decided earlier and thought of not going with all by giving the same answer. Luckily, my answer was correct among all . my Father took this opportunity with great care and helped me to take training on this topic at various places. I am still thankful for the coach who encouraged me and my father who guided me all the way.

Lessons to learn-.

It is fine, not to go with all others..

you are born Unique, so should be your opinion.

Be brave while putting up your opinion. .

Do not fearfully change yourself in order to get accepted by others..

Trust your choices but don't question others..

Encourage others if they are right, even if you are wrong.

WHAT I LEARNED

DAY 1

On the first day we were advised to give each other a positive trait which starts with the initial name of our name and when we were successful in doing so, like FABULOUS FIRDOS, he explained that we should call each other with these names and he explained that when the child is born we most of the time name them with a bad trait which makes the child to accept the negative personality of himself making him a negative person that is why it is important to think of yourself positive as much as possible.

What I learnt is...

What do you think yourself as a person matters the most, there are certain situations where you lose yourself by taking a certain wrong decision but that's surely not a failure. EMOTIONS -

All you have to do is revise and review the situation and feelings you surrounded yourself with and then choose wisely what made you take that decision. What emotions were they and from where did they come from? If the emotion is from yourself that means you need to be emotionally strong

And if that decision is from Satan you need to be spiritually strong. Remember every move, decision and situation has something to make you learn.

DAY 2

When we think extremely positive of oneself we also must take care of thinking positive about others as well because most of the times in order to bring ourself up we usually degrade others which brings up the negative feelings like Envy, Revenge, jealousy which destroys others and at the end oneself too. that is why we must take care that while fulfiling our goal we also must help others so that our goal not only completes but also feels with love.

ACTIVITY - We were given a task of asking our closed ones about our positive and negative traits and when we reached out to our friends some of them hesitated to open up but at the end when we got to know ourself, many of the persons said same negative responses then that must be surely a problem with myself and I need to change it and when I got the same positive responses from many people that means I should keep on going with this activity .this activity was done to bring up the positive energy and to eliminate the negative feelings.

DAY 3

This day was filled with knowledge because on this day we mostly learnt about the knowledge and responsibility where I got to know that without practicing and implementing the knowledge in life the knowledge is useless.

RESPONSIBILITY-

the actual responsibility is not a burden, fault, praise, blame, shame, credit or guilt. infact in responsibility there is no evaluation of good or bad, right or wrong. when you honor what you say that is declaration and at the end what I got to know that - you are not responsible for what people think about you but you are responsible for what you give them to think about you.

If you are responsible then you take charge and account of yourself for every action and try to be a better version of yourself everyday but if you start the blame game then you don't take action and be lazy and at last you become a negative person.

ACTION -

In order to start an ACTION the CONTEXT must be clear as the CORE BASE of an action comes from the context which becomes an INTENTION for a person and the person starts to take it as a BELIEF which makes him a HUMAN being and that's how that changes into an OCCURRENCE which strengthens him to take an actionlet me just put it in a simplified way, like for example if you put earning MONEY as a context you will earn only money and fame as an action and result in this world, but if you put the PARADISE as your context then you will see all the right deeds as an action and result can also be very beneficial for the hereafter as our Islam also gives the more importance to the intention as all the deeds are taken in accordance to the intentions behind it.

The 10 keys of transformation -

1. KNOW WHO YOU ARE - have a self realisation, self consciousness and self awakening of your needs, character and changes.

2. BAGGAGE OF PAST- forgive others by getting rid of all the heartbreak you went through. One can accept the change only when he has a space in his heart to accept the changes.

3. KNOW THE DIFFERENCE - know what is truth or false, what do you prefer most in action your mind or heart, know your ability..etc

4. SUCCESS - purify your heart for success and build the habits and lifestyle accordingly.

5. SATAN - be aware of the whispers, and ignore them.

6. ORGANS- use them wisely like heart to accept the truth, eyes to witness the changes and ears to hear the truth..etc

7. PEACE - one can concentrate only if you are at peace

8. REMOVE VEILS- every one is born pure but growth in life grows veils in eyes too like sins and addiction to it. Removing them is like removing a hurdle.

9. INNER CHANGE - if all the above are followed correctly only then the inner change can be witnessed.

10. HUMAN BEINGS - if all the qualities are present then only a person is a human being.

DAY 4

There are many situations where you have to take a quick decisions and sometimes you take decisions with time but after a certain time after taking a decision if your inner voice of you takes you to the guilt of past or fear of future or rises the questions upon your decision like if/how/why/but then those whispers are clearly from satan which is taking you away from reality.

on this day we learnt about the satan and Adam, everybody knows the story but what conclusions do they give, the whole story of Adam is divided into two paths which every human have that is the path of SUBMISSION and the path of DENIAL.

Prophet Adam choose the path of choice which is submission thereby making him obedient towards his lord, whereas satan denied the path thus giving rise to many feelings of negativity like comparison, superiority, pride, arrogance, revenge, blame, cursing..etc.

How to stop EGO-

Stop taking things personally

Forgive others

Let go and observe.

How the problem leads to self deception -

The man himself creates a problem by a negative feeling and he doesn't realize it and he goes on blaming others for creating a problem and then he starts to lie and insult others which enables him to see a problem created by himself which leads to self deception, a disease which creates and makes the problem huge.

DAY 5

LISTENING is listening till you start to understand and then the filters of interpretation will come giving it a meaning so it is important for a person to build a barrier while listening to filter the words or not there by making complex life into a much simpler one. When one feels difficulty he may feel them in anyone of the two ways which is pain or suffer,

the one who starts to feel pain is when one is treated badly but the one who acts like he is suffered is actually creating it by thinking about the pain continuously. If someone is saying something bad to you what response comes and you accept them as a response creates suffering in your mind.

Choices you have when you do something wrong -

The first way is oftenly noticed, When you do something wrong most of the times we respond in this way either by forgetting it and then rejecting and then giving a justification for the wrong being committed and then repeating it and making it eventually a bad habit so, when person does something wrong he goes on and on by converting the wrong into a sin.

The other way of dealing with the same problem is to acknowledge that and accept that you did something wrong and by not doing it again and then asking forgiveness or repentance and then fully taking responsibility.

Thereby a person who does something wrong but then corrects it by forgiveness can see a huge change in his life. Human and being -At the end of the day we were explained that a human being is a two word combination with a different meaningthe first one is a HUMAN which is the external one which is composed of body and mind, full of physical and mental consciousness responsible for the desires and rational thinkingthe other part of the word is BEING which is internal filled with only the heart which gives rise to spiritual consciousness, realisation, intellectual, distinguished nature etc.

DAY 6

On the 6th day we learnt about the REALITY and PERCEPTION the main difference between the two is reality has no action it only needs to be accepted but the perception is along with shows the action by seeing the reality.

Perception and reality -

Reality is something which is happening in real and the perception is something which you give all by yourself by watching the reality. You are always connected to the heart is the reality but something that happens which disconnects your heart from Allah is the perception.

DAY 7

In every ones life at one point something happens which recreats the future. The man feels bad that the future got affected and things did not go as he expected but one always has to remember that Allah will change you only if you change your way of life which has to be done by changing yourself first which can only happen when the person can start submitting himself to the happenings around from the denial.

World of language -

Everyone has two languages to express one is the MIND which always has the rational thinking which creates the opinion and takes the decision that creates the future.the other one is the heart which is realised thinking which looks upon the reality that makes the mind take the decision.So all one has to do is to commit the decisions with the HEART, changes does not take place when you only declare but when you start to honour and to accept it by your heart then only things starts to change you can do this only by following some of the good deeds like speaking the truth keeping the promise, maintaining the trust, lowering gaze, avoiding the injustice etc.The problem can be solved only when you can change the occurrings we mostly see that whenever we try to solve the problem we can only notice more problems coming into our way and thus making the situation worst so some of the problems cannot be solved, they can be maintained by changing the OCCURRING if you shift the occurrences , new action will occur and if you keep the occurring the same as your previous ones then the same action replays.basically the reality is also filled with real and then illusion. real is the one which is actually happening and illusion is the one which you create into your mind as an illusion leading to run away from the reality which is actually taking place into the outer world.

DAY 8

How you see the problemThere are two ways to see a problem one is by the DESCRIPTIVE way,which is how the problem occurs to you and the other one is the GENERATIVE which is how actually the problem is.descriptive choice mostly leads to the fear and hopelessness and the generative actually makes you strong by looking clearly like a mirror to the problem. Problems can be completely faced with full strength only when one is free from the past guilt and from the fear of future one can empty himself from the future by looking at what binds him and by articulating all the default sayings and then letting go of the past and then start a practical way of looking himself into a better future like planning all of the future and working according to the plan and looking out when the plans don't work.

Every one is a leader of his own life there are only two types of leaders one who thinks only in the box which makes a circle of life there by looking at the humans as objects and taking most of the decisions with the mind and the other leader which looks out of the box has the power to change something and to use his heart when the emotions take over and there by looking at the humans as humans.

DAY 9

On this day we learnt about the EXTERNAL and INTERNAL functions of a human.external is what you feel and internal is what you keep . all of the focus of a human should be on being a BEING instead of doing.

In external life the heart is over the mind and it is a part of outside life where the internal life is the mind over the heart. Whatever the action you take on the external part decision should be thoroughly decided by the internal part so that all of your body concentrates upon the action you are doing. make sure to have your concentration and the focus all at the only one part of your life instead of distributing all your plans at a certain time try to have a time limit on a particular period where all of your energy deals on a particular work so that the work happens perfectly.

Often life gets scattered because one may feel unsuccessful in time division and thus failing in every task, so be focused on one task at a time for all your tasks to be successful.

Day 10

On this day, we were all the certified participants of this course where everyone shared their journey of a change and declared their words as honour to carry forward what they learnt by following them in life.

POEM

we all lay up quick to start our day
Rushing heading all towards pray
Some get busy after that in meditating
Some were silently busy in sleeping.

Then we all are out to walk for a while
morning tea makes everyone smile
Then a moment of chit chat goes on
After the breakfast everybody moves on

A Thousand of moments in every session
everyone showing out their best emotion
we laughed hard and cried a lot
others tears made us to thank Lord

An exercise at middle is good package
To listen to class with calm and courage
break of session is lunch and dinner
An aim is to make everyone a leader

we didn't realise how time passed by
To leave this place everybody deny
yet we have to leave today this peaceful place
To bring learnt things in our living space

from here, we have to part our way of life
we'll be story in each other's life
Hope we'll remember each other wherever we are
smile for moments, spent when we are near

ACTIVITIES

WHAT AM I? -

every workshop has a booklet and an identity card, this workshop too had them. One thing they had was a list of words in a card which read as

I am

Responsible

Accountable

Just

Grateful

Integrity

Generous

Focus on others

These words were asked to repeat after and before session to instill atleast one quality within ourselves.

As what we declare about us , we gradually turn likewise.

MASSAGE-

A day of listening is a day of stress constant hearing may make the person bored , hence, we had a break for relaxation, where we turn around, make a line and give a massage to each other,

On the day one , it was a little embarrassment to let others touch you but by the next time we were quite comfortable and by the end we were ordering each other to massage at shoulders , hands .etc

Alhamdulillah this exercise not only made us fresh but also destroyed the boundaries of the inferiority complex we had.

KNOW YOURSELF THROUGH OTHERS-

After a day of workshop, we were given a task of knowing ourself through others, like we had to call or text the people with whom we usually spend our day with and ask them to send our 3/5 positive and negative traits. Eventually positive was expected but negative were also listed because it was important for every one of us to know where we are going wrong. Same negative response was made to concentrate upon and change it as soon as possible.

The aim was not to look at oneself, it was to look how we are looked at by others.

PAST GUILT-

The session of leaving the guilt of past was held, and as an activity we were asked to hold hands of the person standing beside you, and imagine them as the one who may have you hurted or they might have hurted you and wee were asked to say those words we always imagined to say every now and then. I was shocked to see the woman cry who was holding my hand tight and crying hard. Because my guilt was nothing in front of her. Before I could say something she started to cry in such a way that i couldn't handle her. But Alhamdulillah at last she gathered herself strong and shared her story.

(Her story is shared in other part of the book)

GIFT OTHERS-

Before the end of session, we were asked a day before to bring a gift without mentioning our name on it, just before the end of class, all the gifts were collected and mixed in a bag, and line by line we were asked to pick a gift without even looking.

After a while we were asked to open it, I was so happy to get a sweet Box but the coach at the end said now exchange those gifts with your partner (standing beside). I got a very old book in exchange thought I love sweets but i accepted the book whole heartedly because I love reading books.The main aim of this activity was to be happy for others too, not only for oneself.

POSITIVE NAMING -

We were given a card and a pack of colours and were asked to name oneself with a positive trait with the initial of your name, like Fabulous Firdos ,. ..etc. we were asked to call each other with these name itself till the end of workshop.Unexpectedly repeatedly everyone called me, by this name and a small part of me started to feel that I was actually fabulous, all of a sudden I was feeling loved by everyone which was giving me a positive vibe all around myself and within me making me feel energetic for all the tasks and classes.

Similarly, we label the kids in a negative way like stubborn, fussy...etc which eventually makes the kid to accept himself in a negative way. But if we name our kids with a positive trait they will prove themselves as a positive person.

INTERVIEW OTHERS-

We were given a certain period of time to have a walk with a selected partner in the resort and ask them about their life , when my partner was sharing about herself, all i could see was a spark in her eyes that it was her life she lived and when she was sharing her dreams i could just look at her eyes and say she was extremely proud of herself by going through thick and thin yet standing strong ready to face any storm.When the time was over , and it was my turn to say about my partner, all i could feel her feelings and i don't know why but I was also feeling proud to share her journey like she was my closed one.

Alhamdulillah although it was just the first day of my dys journey but it built a connection like I knew her from years.I still miss her and love her for the sake of Allah .

MEDITATION -

Atleast of 15 minutes silence was maintained by every participant to freshen up the mind and get ready to gather the knowledge, one can also hear adhan, or any Quranic verses to maintain the concentration.

DRAW WHAT YOU LEARNT-

At the end of each day , every participant was asked to draw something which depicts what he learnt from the session, the sheet was given with two sections namely after and before to ensure there were some changes made by the listener and has decided to change something about his own life.(Some of the amazing drawings are discussed in next chapters)

PHYSICAL EXERCISE -

A day started with physical exercise is a day going to be healthy, i initially skipped the sessions because I was sleepy, but after two days I joined because they had an arrangement of tea , and am extremely thankful to Allah that I attended the tea time talks as the practical of what we learnt can be seen there and I met some wonderful people over there .

LISTENING -

A piece of newspaper was given to one among the two participants, one had to read and the other had to listen and repeat it, and the second chance was given to the one who was hearing earlier, but during this practice we saw we made immense mistakes in repeating the news we heard a second before, the words were altered giving the same meaning but the coach asked to repeat the words in the same way we heard,

At the end , i learnt that our ear hears but within fraction of second our mind starts to give the meaning thereby altering words which is a very common factor between humans to cause problems.

POP THE BALLOON-

Every participant was given a balloon to blow, and a pin was handed over to each and they gave us a minute of time and said whosoever saves his balloons from popping is the winner and within a minute everyone tried to burst the balloon and atlast none of them managed to save the balloon.

But later we realised if we have stood quiet by holding our respective balloons we could have saved each other but the pin we had gave our mind an idea of destroying others and creating a feeling of revenge on opposite ones and thus we loose and others too.

In this world we have to win by taking others too on this path, we can't expect success by letting others fail.

CROSS THE GLASS-

A set of glasses were arranged alternately with a space of a feet between and there were few objects placed, few teams were made one among them should be blindfolded and the other team mates have to lead him to enter into the glass section and pick up the object, this game was purely based on the trust the blindfolded person had on his teammates.I still remember that I got no positive points and we lost with many negative points.

CHAT AT TEA-

A tea break was arranged twice in a day, and whatever we learnt, we discussed, that time was merely a magical moment among all those sessions because same topic but many opinions and perspectives were Heard and i learnt a single topic with atleast 20 different perspectives, this time was the time to make our mind to know others opinion on a single topic as well.

AN MOTIONAL BREAKDOWN -

We started our day by having a partner and a few seconds were carried out daily to look at each others eyes and build a contact of trust , and at the end of session these eye contacts gave much more deeper meaning to the silence we maintained during this time

At first contact our eyes wandered, after some meetings and contacts we searched some feelings in our partner's eyes, but as these contacts came to an end , the heart was longing for some more contacts but eventually it end in such a way that every one of them cried without any reason.

We all miss each other and those magical eye contacts like whispering about our life to each other without speaking.

MAGICAL MOMENTS

1.

Before attending a 10 days workshop, as i already mentioned, I attended a 3 day workshop with my mother in Hyderabad , i usually don't like travelling but those 3 days changed me in a way that led my mind open to face new challenges Earlier, I used to get irritated by my mother and her presence was making me feel embarassed until i learnt about reality and perspective i had about her and i thought to change it Because my behaviour was Surely making her upset, i was feeling guilty for not having my father with me, i was feeling angry because she couldn't speak english and was trying to talk to new people in urdu, I failed to notice she was learning, just like me.

I still feel bad for my behaviour but Alhamdulillah at last everything changed. i promised myself to accept my mother for how she is. And i am proud to have her, because since the day i was born she took great care of me and i know she'll always continue doing so.

LESSONS -.

Accept your parents as they are..

Express your love towards your parents often..

The most important form of love is to respect..

Whenever your parents get hurt by your behaviour, ask forgiveness as soon as possible..

Hurting your parents, doesn't guarantee you happiness in life too.

2.

when i was in in hyderabad, with my mother for the workshop, we reached hotel and there we saw a guy with a very messy appearance, he was about to checkout from the room we booked. so we stayed until he did so, the manager asked him about the advanced money but the guy replied that he paid it earlier. this conversation turnd up into a heated arguement. me and my mother thought the guy must be lying until the manager arrived and checked the footage and saw that the guy paid. The manager asked forgiveness & let him go. this taught us a lesson that the appearance has nothing to do with the character.

LESSONS -.

Do not make a perception without knowing the Reality..

Character has nothing to do with the physical appearance..

Not all perceptions are wrong, but recheck before terming it as reality..

Reality is what actually is, and the perception is what you think that to be..

Treat others according to the reality not according to your perception.

3.

on the first day every participant was provided with an identity card and a diary to write notes in . I didnt even opened the given diary, my co-participant asked me about this, i said "my elder sister loves writing in diaries, so I am keeping this as a gift for her," and i was writing my points in my other notebook. Till the end of the day, she called me and gave me another diary by saying "your diary is a gift for your sister, let this diary be a gift for you. from me" I thanked her for this kind gesture.

LESSONS -.

Try to gift others often..

Gifting others makes your heart happy..

Be thankful for the person you received your gift from..

It is not important to gift only the people you know..

if you see someone is in need of something try to help them.

4.

At the end of everyday session, every participant had to share what they learnt, and on the first day i wrote a poem and everyone loved it and encouraged me to the extent that today i wrote two books of my poems today.I still think of the day as the most blessed one because whatever you learn is waste until you follow and it was pretty visible in the way everyone encouraged me by clapping and asked me to continue itA news reporter who was a participant Published my poem in the magazine and i felt extremely proud of myself, blessed by my lord, And grateful for this talent I am also thankful for my father who let me carry on my talent and everyone who encouraged me by listening to my poems.

LESSONS -.

Your Little encouragement can help others to achieve their aim..

Do not degrade or defame other's talent..

Appreciate others talent instead of being jealous..

Learn to help others even if it saying a kind word or gesture..

Try to showcase your talent without thinking about others.

5.

My father and i were all prepared for the ten days workshop, my father after reaching out their didn't wanted to attend as he thought i would not feel open to share, but k made a deal that let's just live as participants and he agreed.later , for the Starting 4 days, i saw my father trying hard to understand the english language and the conversation . i saw him feeling sleepy and ignored. I still remember that it was the fourth day, i could not see him in that state any longer, l left my class, heading to my room, made ablution and prayed for half an hour. crying & praying to Allah that "o my lord, he stayed here because i requested him and he has paid from the amount he worked hard and i can't see it getting wasted, o Allah my father loves to learn, please open all the doors of knowledge for him and allow him to learn in the easiest way" . I ended the prayer and Alhamdulillah, after the break, i noticed that every session had urdu and english language too. I couldn't believe that my supplication was accepted so soon. my father is my strength who loves to read and learn. I still think of that day, that how my heart craved to run towards my lord, to pray for my father.

LESSONS -.

Pray if your heart is constantly asking for it..

Pray for your loved ones often..

Pray , supplicate and never lose hope .

Sometimes, things change only when you supplicate..

Miracles happen only when you try hard for it.

6.

on the fourth day of workshop, i still remember that i gathered all the strength to share my story, where i was struggling, to get over it. My father's brother was very ill, and he asked me to to come over for a talk, i was quite busy that day yet i went to have a look at him. when he came to know that i was appointed as a teacher, he said "yeah, yeah! why will you come to meet me when you are so busy in your life" & i got so angry by hearing & thinking that he was being ungrateful & i left the house without greeting. A month later; the news came that he was no more and my heart broked. I was filled with guilt that out of my arrogance, i didn't talked to him and i carried that guilt with me for over a year, until the day of workshop , i was crying so hard that my father hugged me and consoled me to the extent that he couldn't believe how much i was holding it inside. I am still thankful because i never hugged my father till that day and I felt that every single tear of my guilt was making me free by getting out.

LESSONS -.

The more you carry your guilt, the more it aches your heart..

When you feel it's heavy, make your heart lighter by putting out .If you can't express your pain, let your tears do so..

Only your loved ones knows how to console you..

Check on your loved ones often for the emotional support.

7.

There were a group of lecturers from AL-AMEEN college kolkata, who were attending the workshop as participants. I always asked those lecturers "why is this choclate so chocolaty" & we all shared a great laughter. on this, A few days later, i was tryng to have a tamarind from tree & out of nowhere a lecturer helped me. while he was busy in phone I thanked him and shared the tamarind with everyone. on the last day of workshop, the lecturer called me on stage and said "this young girl, aged 20 is energetic, talkative, friendly and sweet just as the choclate she eats everyday, she reminds me of my sister whom i lost a year before andi Still miss her, but when i saw this girl, u always remember her, i just pray that may this girl have a beautiful life ahead." I got very emotional that someone lost their loved ones. and trying their best to be happy and am grateful that Allah made me a reason for people like them to smile.

LESSONS -.

Respect others emotions..

Try to be the way you are..

Carry a cheerful smile because you have it..

Let your smile brighten your day and others as well.

8.There was a worker in the resort we stayed during workshop, we had an hour long break after lunch and she used to come to clean the pool everyday. I used to sit near the pool and watch the fishes running around and i loved talking with her, she and I used to have a minute chat daily. And on the last day of my workshop, i met her and said goodbye and hugged her to the extent that we had tears in our eyes . And at that moment, there came a man, who witnessed this was invited by my dad to the workshop and my my action made him to attend that day till the end, my dad was very happy when the man said that to my father by pointing out to me but i was not aware of this. later, when we reached home, my father said "That hug of yours to a cleaner has cleaned heart of my heart"

LESSONS -.

Do not talk according to their profession..

Let your emotion be true like your heart..

Do not degrade others if you are blessed more..

Do not be arrogant of yourself.

9.

One of the moments, i cherish is when i saw a group of foreigners wearing traditional saree, and helped them in letting it handle. they thanked me but the moment to admire was when one of them whom i helped wished me luck for the future as she was leaving the resort, i was sitting at aCorner applying henna she asked how beautiful is this, you drew it very well" . I asked"you want to try?" she was extremely happy and i could clearly read her face with shiny eyes showing how much she enjoyed itAt last, she said. "i will forever cherish this moment and am going to remember your face for life because i love Indian tradition." whatever it is always carry your culture and share it.

LESSONS -.

Carry your culture wherever you are..

Be proud of your culture and share it..

Introduce your culture with love and respect.

10.The sessions of break during the workshop days were with everyone who were present at the resort. being an

Indian, there is always an excitement when you See foreigners, i always used to sit and chat with one or other. I met an old man whom i helped and he said, to me "you are a very energetic girl that made me happy because i love to pass on the positive vibes"

I also met a woman to whom i always greeted but couldn't talk much with her, this continued till a day, when i was extremely sad and during that break i yet managed to wish her, and she said " i always see you as a very cheerful lady that makes my day." that woman who I see only Smiles back whenever I wish and never utters a word other than that, but what she said was making me feel like, all those positive vibes were calling me for more energy. however, i loved whatever those moments were spent with her.

LESSONS -.

Greet others with a smile..

A smile costs nothing to share..

However your day was , you deserve a smile of happiness for yourself.

11.

I met a woman who was a lawyer by profession. she was always friendly and a bit childish joking often how she could have been a mother today with a child of my age & we would often laugh about it. I still remember the day she opened up about her tragic past life of being raised by a her grandmother whom she loved so much

But, a dispute of words led her to leave her grandmother alone for a while and upon returning back she was shattered to see her dead. she explained how the horrific past still haunts her and the satan influences her to die every minute and blames her for her grandmother's death. she was crying Inconsolably, and after the workshop of that day, i was confused about how to approach her because she was smiling till the day but i didn't knew what to say that would console her . As what she experienced I never thought of going through something like that But eventually the way she let the words out calmed her heart and she was the one who came & hugged me by saying the same joke I was in a state of shock that how strong was she and for how long was she holding it & I still call her often to check on her. I always pray for her that may she live hapy forever and in hereafter too.

LESSONS -.

If you see someone happy doesn't mean they are..

When you hear someone's sad past then learn from it .

Be thankful if you hear someone's suffering that God saved you from this suffering.

12.

I met a woman in my workshop, she wasn't a Part of it. yet she came with her two kids. I initiated the conversation with her because there was no other person to interact with. she said she didn't give her children the wordly education instead she is making them learn arabic and was doing homeschooling. i thought it would be difficult for kids to live without competing in this world. A while later, All of us participants went out for a break and the task was to climb a mountain we were on a talk and all of a sudden i saw the woman with hijab with her kids all alone letting the kids climb the mountain, first i thought it was weird because that was not a place for the kids to climb and there was no safety but from the highest view all i could see was a fighter woman climbing behind her kids asking them to climb alone without holding her hand. I still don't know, who she is, because she never lifted up her hijab, but i still pray for her and her kids As what she thought of giving is something that this worldly education fails to give.Today as a mother i feel what amount of courage a woman needs to stand at the opposite of this cruel world to teach the kids humanity & religion.

LESSONS -.

Learn to teach your kids religion first .

A mother is the first teacher..

Provide the righteous knowledge for your kids..

Teach the best of religion for kids first..

Let your kids live their life with religion as it's foundation.

13.

I attended a workshop, where i saw a woman with hijab but a high camel hump I tried to talk but couldn't, At the breaki heard her elder sister advising her about hadith, where prophet said camel hump as a warning sign of

Qiyamah. And i thought not to intervene but still she had the hump till the day. The next day, i saw her face with some marks on it, so, i thought she Covered her because face of it. At the end of workshop. i saw her and her hijab was properly pinned without a hump, i looked at her and said she was really looking beautiful and she smiled back which started a good conversation between us.

LESSONS -.

know the matter in detail before judging. .

Do not be harsh about other's character..

Advise in a way which sounds good..

choose good words to advise..Do not advise repeatedly..

Encourage and appreciate when someone does good act

Have a comfortable conversation before advising people whom you don't know.

14.

I met a man named Khalid, in workshop ofBangalore, he usually had conversation during tea time in morning and once i joined them on my father's advice. Khalid sir initiated the Conversation by saying that he met a man. who said i'm really happy, have luxurious Cars, bungalow- etc so, he asked where are those?" The man replied "i can't bring them here", so khalid sir responded how can you be happy, when these arent with you here. "The man stood stunned because those materialistic things brought him happiness and he would be sad if those were lost. khalid sir gave a beautiful answer that "happiness is what you carry every where. happiness lives within you safely which doesn't depend on anything on anything or any person"

LESSONS -

• your happiness should not be dependent

Happiness lies in your heart only by being

Contented.

• By being happy you make yourself & others happy .

Happiness has no scale to measure except feelings..

Let your happiness increase by sharing..

You will fail miserably if you try to find happiness in the worldly materials.

ABOUT THE COACH

About the coach-

Born in 1950, Sadathullah Khan studied Science and Engineering in Bangalore, and then branched off in a different direction--first in the world of business, then followed by journalism, and then guiding people discover a purpose in their lives!That is how Sadath's journey with the Discover Yourself Workshop began. Designed by Sadath himself, this unique three-day educational workshop is a journey to know oneself. It is a unique experiential and empowering programme that purports to transform you into a positive-thinking person. It seeks to remind people of the need to connect to the Creator, which alone is the means to enkindle love, happiness, contentment, pence as well success in this life and the Hereafter. Participants realize that the source of peace is God! A man with a mission who has dedicated his life to serving humanity, 35000+ people across worldwide have benefited from his Discover Yourself workshop of different nationalities, background, and faithIn his workshop, he engages with people to empower them through self-introspection and by promoting the concept of Discover Yourself (To know one's True Self), which helps in getting a breakthrough in one's Personal and Professional life. Since 2002, he has conducted over 400 three-day workshops, in Asia, US,

Middle East, Europe and Africa which has brought about significant positive changes in the lives of thousands of participants. He is also honored with Doctorate in Personal Excellence & Life Mastery with specialization in Transformation Leadership. His life's vision is to nurture leaders with an ability to make a difference and an innate capability to empower, inspire and lead humanity to the path of truth, love, and peace.Organizing Sadathullah Khan's Three Day Discover Yourself' Workshop is simple, Even a common man can schedule without any hassle. Just go through Discover Yourself Website (www.discoveryourself in) and once convinced Email your request and he will come back to you within a week time. [Note: There is no fees to the organizer for organizing workshop, except managing travel, stay and similar expenses for Saduthullah Klan and managing your 50-300 of audiences and their logistics)

List of Contributors

The other books written by the author are-
GOLDEN ADVISE OF PARENTS
HALAL LOVE STORIES
RAMADAN a blessed month
10 gems of luqman
DEPRESSION
Unsaid feelings
The 50 life lessons
Islamic lullabies
You can follow the author on social media as-
Nabi_e_ummah on Instagram
Or
Charge_ur_eemaan on Instagram
Or
www.firdosetarannum@gmail.com

Notes

In the name of Allah with Whose name nothing can harm on earth or in heaven, and He is the All-Hearing, All-Knowing

O Allah, You are my Lord, there is no god but You, in You I put my trust, and You are Lord of the mighty Throne. Whatever Allah wills happens, and whatever Allah does not will does not happen. There is no power and no strength except with Allah, the Most High, the Most Great. I know that Allah has power to do all things and that Allah has encompassed all things by His knowledge. O Allah, I seek refuge with You from the evil of my own self, and the evil of every creature that You hold by its forelock. Verily my Lord is on a straight path

O Allaah, Lord of Jibreel (Gabriel), Michael and Israfeel, Creator of the heavens and the earth, Knower of the unseen and the seen, You are the Knower of the unseen and the seen, You will judge between Your slaves concerning that wherein they differ. Guide me to the truth of that wherein they differed by Your leave, for You guide whomsoever You will to the Straight Path

O Allah, help me, guide me, correct me, enable me to attain what is right and earn reward, and forgive me if I make a mistake or am deprived of an answer.

O my Lord! Open for me my chest (grant me self-confidence, contentment, and boldness); And ease my task for me; And make loose the knot (the defect) from my tongue, (i.e. remove the incorrectness from my speech), That they understand my speech

-Aameen

Made in the USA
Monee, IL
07 July 2026

56553621R00031